The
Great Tribulation
and the
Resurrection

John Johnson

PAGE PUBLISHING
Conneaut Lake, PA

First originally published by Page Publishing 2024

All chapters and scriptures marked and unmarked
are taken from the King James Version Bible.

ISBN 979-8-88793-559-1 (pbk)
ISBN 979-8-88793-571-3 (digital)

Printed in the United States of America

PREFACE

Hello! I thank God for you so much for buying this book and reading it. My name is John Johnson, and I have been a servant of my Lord and Savior, Jesus Christ, for years. I like to thank Him for giving me the permission to write this book on the Great Tribulation. This is a book on great insight on the events that will happen in the Tribulation.

My foster parents were devoted Christians. No, they were not perfect—even I was not perfect and still not perfect. But being a Christian is a journey in life. The Christian will grow in faith and, as time goes on, become the man and woman they are supposed to be in Christ. I would like to say this is a great opportunity to share to the reader the things that will take place in the Great Tribulation in the near future.

At the beginning of the tribulation, an apocalypse event will take place until the end of the tribulation. Apocalypse is an event involving destruction or damage on an awesome or catastrophic scale (Oxford Language Dictionary). The books of Daniel and Revelation predict certain times that war will take place. Some scholars believe that world war three will happen then the beginning of the seven year peace treaty will happen which will be the start of the Great Tribulation. But the holy Bible tells you what will happen. The start of the Great Tribulation the peace treaty will happen, and in the middle of the peace treaty the Antichrist will break this treaty. For when they shall say peace and safety, then sudden destruction cometh up on them, as travail upon a woman with child, and they shall not escape. 1 Thessalonians 5:3 KJV. Abomination and desolation will happen at the temple mount in Jerusalem. After Iran and their allies attack the antichrist and their armies which is Germany and the

10 nations from the European Union. World war three will happen and at the end of the tribulation, nation will gather at Armageddon where they will be led to the valley of Jehoshaphat by Jesus Christ and the resurrected saints. Jesus Christ will return first to resurrect the saints. Then He will return to earth with the saints, which are His army, and take care of the armies that fight against Christ upon His return, which will be the Antichrist and his army and the nations that worship the beast.

Read about what happened to the devil and what the saints will do in the millennium for a thousand years. Read about the battle with Israel as Russia, and China will attack this nation after the millennium. Finally, see what happens with the new heaven and new earth. What an exciting and wonderful revelation! Bible prophecy has extreme information that pertains to the last days, and we are in the last days. "Blessed is he that readeth and they that hear the words of this prophecy and keep those things which are written therein: for the time is at hand" (Revelation 1:3). A person needs to respond to Bible prophecy in obedience to be a doer, not just hear the Word, because God's final hour is near.

INTRODUCTION

Most preachers, prophets, and evangelists believe that Jesus Christ will return before the great tribulation begins, so Jesus Christ's second coming will result in mankind almost wiping themselves off the face of the earth by using nuclear weapons. But if a person reads the Bible very carefully with an open mind (not what you personally believe in), asking God to give you wisdom and understanding on this matter, it will be very clearly an indication to a person that the season is very close for Jesus Christ's return after the tribulation. "And except those days should be shortened, there should no flesh be saved: but for the elect's sake (saints) those days shall be shortened" (Matthew 24:22). Matthew 24:29–31 explains it very well.

Before that great day of the resurrection, many astounding events must take place on earth. The seven-year tribulation will be a result from the rejection of Jesus Christ's salvation. "And because iniquity shall abound, the love of many shall wax cold" (Matthew 24:12). Mankind shall become worse and worse, taking heed to seducing spirits (being evil in the sight of God); as a result, many will face disasters and destruction during the great tribulation (the action or process of causing so much damage to something that it no longer exists or cannot be repaired) Oxford Language Dictionary. But Jesus will take care of those who are faithful in serving Him. He will keep them in a safe place and provide their every need. But those who are lukewarm toward God (not serving him with a whole heart) will suffer persecution and some will be killed. When studying the Holy Bible there are many commentary books, history books, secular history books that a person can line up with Bible prophecy to get the correct answer to a particular scripture that a person doesn't understand. But be careful with certain commentary books because I found out they can be misleading.

FACT OR FICTION?

In today's society, the majority of people have their own perception of who God really is. The Holy Bible gives you an indication who God really is. So why are there so many different religions in the world today? Well, the devil plays a major role in this.

In the book of Revelation, the last book written by John (the book of prophecy), Revelation 12:9 states, "And the great dragon spoke was cast out, that old serpent, called the Devil, and Satan, which deceiveth the whole world: he was cast out into the earth, and his angels were cast out with him." Revelation 12:7–9 spoke about war in heaven.

Ever since the beginning of the world (mankind), Satan, and his angels has influenced man to rebel against God's commandments, statutes, and laws. God is not the author of confusion but of sound wisdom, understanding, and peace. It is the devil who causes confusion. Read 1 Corinthians 14:33 KJV. It states that God is not the God of confusion but of order. Satan will attack a person's mind to have them believe in anything that is contrary to God's Word. All through the Old Testament, God would give the nation of Israel chances to repent from their sins, serving false gods; and if they didn't, He would punish them for their rebellion.

"For thou shalt worship no other god: for the Lord, whose name is Jealous, is a jealous God" (Exodus 34:14 KJV).

God commanded for His people to serve Him and Him only. After all, God created us and the world—serving false gods and idols is very disrespectful to him (formidable). God deserves complete respect, and we should honor Him with a whole heart. Serving Him with our heart, might, and mind.

"Thou are worthy, O Lord, to receive glory and honor and power: for thou has created all things, and for thy pleasure, they are and were created" (Revelation 4:11).

"Thou shall have none other gods before me" (Deuteronomy 5:7).

God gave complete instructions in the Holy Scriptures not to worship or bow down to false gods. All through the Scriptures, it mentions God is a merciful and loving God, but you really don't want to get on God's bad side.

"(For the Lord thy God is a jealous God among you) lest the anger of the Lord thy God be kindled against thee, and destroy thee from off the face of the earth" (Deuteronomy 6:15).

Ephesians 4:5–6 in the New Testament of the Holy Scriptures indicates in verse five "one Lord, one faith, one baptism" and in verse six "one God and Father of all, who is above all, and through all, and in you all."

There are many religions today, just to name a few: Buddhism, Hinduism, Atheism, Indigenous, Judaism, Christianity, Islam, etc. I will talk about what, I believe, are the two popular beliefs on earth today (there are three most important, but I will focus on two), Christianity and Islam.

In the Christian beliefs, we have what is known as the Roman Catholic church, Presbyterian, Lutheran, Methodist, Baptist, Episcopal, Pentecost, and Apostolic churches. Each one has their own set of standard beliefs that are separated from one another. But the book of Acts in the Holy Bible makes it very clear that there is only one way to be saved.

Acts 4:10–12 states,

> Be it known unto you all, and to all the people of Israel, that by the name of Jesus Christ of Nazareth, whom ye crucified, whom God raised from the dead, even by him doth this man stand here before you whole.

> This is the stone which was set at nought
> of you builders, which is become the head of the
> corner.
> Neither is there salvation in any other: for
> there is none other name under heaven given
> among men, whereby we must be saved.

The Islam religion, which has millions of followers, doesn't believe that Jesus Christ is the Savior of the world. They reject the Jewish people who are God's chosen people. They believe the prophet Muhammad is the Savior of the world. There are two Islam faiths, each one believes in something different.

Islam has millions of followers in the Midwest and United States. The Jews, Islamic people, and the Christians in the Middle East are fighting over who has the rights to the Temple Mount in Jerusalem. But of course, we know Judaism is important too because the Jews are God's chosen people, and everything centers around the nation of Israel. The Temple Mount—to the Jews, Islamic, and Christians—is seen as the third most holy site on earth. That is why they are continually in conflict of the Temple Mount. It is regarded as where God's presence is manifested in a powerful way. It is where the Jews go and pray all the time.

Muslims believe this is where the prophet Muhammad ascended to heaven. Islamic people believe there is no God but Allah. Muslims believe he created the world in six days and sent prophets such as Noah, Abraham, Moses, David, Jesus, and lastly, Muhammad who called people to worship him, rejecting idolatry and polytheism.

Ali (Arabic: علي, ʿAlī) is a male Arabic name derived from the Arabic root ʿ-l-w, which literally means "high, elevated, or champion." Islamic traditional use of the name goes back to the Islamic leader ʿAlī ibn Abī Ṭālib, but the name is also present among some pre-Islamic Arabs (e.g., Banu Hanifa and some rulers of Saba and Himyar) and identical in form and meaning to the Hebrew עֵלִי, Eli, which goes back to the high priest Eli in the biblical Books of Samuel.

There's Only One Way to Inherit the Kingdom of God

The devil knows his future will be the lake of fire at the end. He is trying to persuade as many people as possible to miss the mark, which is eternal life with Jesus Christ. Satan will bring all types of thoughts (lies) to stop a person from accepting Jesus Christ in their life.

In John 3:5 KJV, it says, "Jesus answered, Verily, verily, I say unto thee, Except a man be born of water and of the Spirit, he cannot enter into the kingdom of God." This is the only way to make it in heaven. You must repent (Godly sorry, turn away from those things that are contrary to His Word, and have a change of heart) for living a sinful life against the Almighty God, Our Lord and Savior, Jesus Christ. Then you will receive the gift of the Holy Spirit.

Once this happens, people will notice you are not the same. You will speak like a Godly person having peace and joy in your daily walk with Christ. You will have a total desire to serve Jesus Christ. Once you study daily the Word of God, you will start to have the characteristics of God, which are peace, joy, patience, long-suffering, and love.

"Then Peter said unto them, Repent, and be baptized (immersed in water) every one of you in the name of Jesus Christ for the remission of sins (forgiveness), and ye shall receive the gift of the Holy Ghost" (Acts 2:38).

Jesus said, "Verily, verily, I say unto you, He that entereth not by the door into the sheepfold, but climbeth up some other way, the same is a thief and a robber" (John 10:1).

There is only one way to make it in heaven and that is Jesus Christ's way. Any other way he has taken is away from God's true way in entering heaven.

Once you accept Jesus Christ in your life, you must keep God's commandments, statutes, and laws. No, it's not going to be easy sometimes, but your mind has to be focused on Jesus. Yes, you will make mistakes in life being a Christian; this is why you need to read and study the Bible and pray to God He will give you the necessary strength to make it (overcome) in Christ. So it will be a battle at times, but always keep your focus on His Word and lean not to your own understanding. This is where we get in trouble because doubt will set in before we know it, and we'll be saying and doing things that's not God's way of doing things. But if you don't have His Holy Spirit, how can you follow Him the true way?

"Many will say to me in that day (day of judgement), Lord, Lord, have we not prophesied in thy name? And in thy name have cast out devils? And in thy name done many wonderful works? And then will I profess unto them, I never knew you: depart from me, ye that work iniquity" (Matthew 7:22–23).

Imagine, on that day, you're thinking in your mind, *I did all I can to serve God*, and He says depart from me, I never knew you. What a frightening day that will be—being thrown into the lake of fire. You thought you were serving the true God, but it was counterfeit all the time. In the book of John, Jesus said, "And ye shall know the truth, and the truth shall make you free" (John 8:32).

A person must humble themselves and seek God fully for understanding and wisdom. One of the ways of doing this correctly is to stop listening to every person who says they are a prophet of God. Search the Scriptures for yourself. Matthew 18:3 says, "Verily, I say unto you, Except ye be converted, and become as little children, ye shall not enter into the kingdom of heaven." This does not mean physically become like a child but mentally (humble yourselves) being like Christ so you can see things like Christ sees them. This is the way a person can be effective in the kingdom of God. The person can serve God with all their heart because not remaining humble, the person can get off track in serving God. Before you know it, he/she will become lukewarm (compromising) with their faith in God. This can eventually have a Christian fall away from church. The Christian will become confused and lose out on the Christian values and teachings of Jesus Christ.

"Know ye not that the unrighteous shall not inherit the kingdom of God? Be not deceived: neither fornicators, nor idolators, nor adulterers, nor effeminate, nor abusers of themselves with mankind, Nor thieves, nor covetous, nor drunkards, no revilers, nor extortioners, shall inherit the kingdom of God" (1 Corinthians 6:9–10). Definition of these words check oxford language dictionary, Merriam Webster dictionary online.

> Fornication: having sexual intercourse between people not married to each other.
> Idolater: a person who worship an idol or idols.
> Adultery: voluntary sexual intercourse between a married person and a person who is not his or her spouse.
> Effeminate: is embodiment of traits in a boy or man that more often associated with feminine behavior.
> Abusers of themselves with mankind: one who lies with a male as with a female, sodomite, homosexual.
> Thieves: criminal who takes property belonging to someone else with the intention of keeping it or selling it.
> Covetous: greedy, very desirous.
> Drunkards: a person who is habitually drunk.
> Revilers: verbal abuse.
> Extortioners: criminal who extorts money from someone by threatening to expose embarrassing information about them.

Galatians 5:19–21 verses 19- now the works of the flesh are manifest, which are these: adultery fornication, uncleanness, lasciviousness. 20- idolatry, witchcraft, hatred, variance, emulations, wrath, strife, seditions, heresies. 21- envying, murders, drunkenness, revellings, and such like: of which I tell you before, as 1 have also told you in time past, that they which do such things shall not inherit the kingdom of God.

> Sexual immorality: all unlawful sexual intercourse. It includes adultery, prostitution, sexual relations between unmarried individuals, homosexuality, and bestiality.
> Impurity: the condition of being impure.
> Debauchery: excessive indulgence in sensual pleasures.
> Enmity: the state or feeling of being actively opposed or hostile to someone or something.
> Rivalries: competition for same objections or for superiority in the same field.
> Dissension: disagreement that leads to discord.
> Orgies: wild party especially involving excessive drinking and unrestrained sexual activity.

"For fornicators, for sodomites, for kidnappers, for liars, for perjurers, and if there is any other thing that is contrary to sound doctrine" (1 Timothy 1:10). Sodomy is a sexual intercourse involving anal or oral copulation.

Matthew 12:31–32 talk about every sin and blasphemy against the spirit be forgiven men, but blasphemy against the Spirit will not be forgiven men. If anyone speaks a word against the son of man (Jesus), it will be forgiven; but whoever speaks against the Holy Spirit, it will not be forgiven either in this age or in the age to come. No matter how much you attempt to repent or confess your sins to God, you will not enter heaven. Blasphemy is speaking evil of God or toward Him personally. This will include the Christian who willfully rejects Jesus's Spirit and remains in rebellion against God. God will no longer have His spirit dwell in him.

The number one sin, I believe, that would have a Christian conduct themselves like this is bitterness. Bitterness makes a person hold strife and resentment in their heart. The more time a person holds on to bitterness, the more anger will build up in a person's life. This will make a person unable to forgive. Before you know it, the person's attitude becomes contrary to God because of their anger, and the person will start to speak in a harsh way. Don't let the root of bitterness enter your heart. Get rid of it because it will and can destroy your life and others you love. Ephesians 4:31–32 basically speak about getting rid of bitterness, wrath, anger, clamor, evil speaking, and all malice be put away. Be kind to one another because Christ has forgiven you.

"Then came Peter to him, and said, Lord, how oft shall my brother sin against me, and I forgive him? Till seven times? Jesus said unto him, I say not unto thee, Until seven times: but, Until seventy times seven (490 times)" (Matthew 18:21–22).

Wow! Jesus is really serious about this. When reading and studying the Bible, you will notice everything in the Scriptures is to help us grow as Christians. Remember, no one is perfect. It takes time to have a successful Christian life. Living a Christian life is like taking a journey (experience ups and downs). Philippians 4:13 KJV says, "I can do all things through Christ which strengthens me." By leaning on Jesus, He will give you strength to overcome many obstacles.

SALVATION FOR EVERYBODY

The flesh cannot inherit the kingdom of God.

"Now this I say, brethren, that flesh and blood cannot inherit the Kingdom of God; neither doth corruption inherit incorruption" (1 Corinthians 15:50 KJV). Serving sin will only bring shame and death in your life (spiritually).

"If we confess our sins, he is faithful and just to forgive us our sins, and to cleanse us from all unrighteousness" (1 John 1:9 KJV).

If you are determined to stop doing the same sin, God will give you the grace to overcome it. Sometimes, Christians will make up things and say, "I don't have the strength to stop doing something." That's because they don't want to stop doing that particular thing that makes them feel good. That sin they are committing will result in iniquity. Iniquity is gross injustice or wickedness. If a person increase in their sins, it will become iniquity. The person will be at a very dangerous state. That person will be on dangerous ground with God. That person can receive a terrible punishment from God.

But in 1 Corinthians 10:13 KJV, it says, "There hath no temptation taken you but such as is common to man: but God is faithful, who will not suffer you to be tempted above that ye are able; but will with the temptation also make a way to escape, that ye may be able to bear it." That sin that seems like it's impossible to get it out of your life may require you to fast and pray for several days. Fasting can help you greatly because you're bringing the flesh under submission. Wherever the sin may be yesterday's sin, today's sin, or an old sin, fasting will break that barren and set you free from some things that are not pleasing to God. The Bible indicates salvation is for everyone no matter what you have done in life. God loves you. John 3:15 KJV states, "That whosoever believeth in him should not perish, but have eternal life." God truly loves you. In John 3:17 KJV, Jesus stated, "For God sent not his Son into the world to condemn the world; but that the world through him might be saved."

THE FOUR HORSEMEN—
THE APOCALYPSE

Apocalypse: the complete final destruction of the world. An event involving destruction of the world. An event involving destruction or damage on an awesome or catastrophic scale.

Revelation 6:1–8 KJV speaks about the first four seals out of seven seals. The first horseman pertains to the Antichrist (white horse). He will come to be a dictator and deceive many in his one-world government starting with Europe and the Middle East, then the world. I will discuss more details of him further in the book.

Verse four talks about a red horseman, the second seal. He will be given power to take peace from the earth that they should kill one another. Jesus stated in Matthew 24:6 that there will be wars or rumors of wars. This horseman will start World War III. World Wars I and II will be nothing in comparison to this war. This will be a global war. Nuclear weapons will be involved in this event.

Verses five to six represent the third seal, which is the black horse. He that sat on him had a pair of balance in his hands. Because of the horrific events, God will bring upon the earth a world war III; there is going to be a tremendous food and water shortage. The food that is available will be hard to get. Starvation will be at a scale that no one can imagine.

Verses seven to eight, the fourth seal, represents the pale horse. Death and hell followed him, and he will kill with a sword and with hunger.

The Great Tribulation

There are so many preachers, authors, and commentators who has given an idea on how the great tribulation will happen. But what does the Bible really say about the seven-year great tribulation? Things will get bad here on earth. It will be so difficult and miserable, and disasters will be happening around the world. It will be a time of suffering more than anyone can imagine. I believe there will be an oil conflict in the Middle East that will have the south (Iran and their allies) attack the north (Germany and the Holy Roman Empire) that will be stationary in Jerusalem in the Middle East.

"And at that time of the end shall the king of the south push at him (attack): and the king of the north shall come against him like a whirlwind (surround him), with chariots, and with horsemen, and with many ships; and he shall enter the countries, and shall overflow and pass over" (Daniel 11:40).

This is the king of the south: Iran and Muslim nations. The kings of the north will be Germany and the Holy Roman Empire armies. But what will happen? As you can see in Daniel 11:44, it states, "But tiding out of the east (China) and that of the north (Russia) shall trouble him, therefore, he shall go forth with great fury to destroy and utterly to make away many." This will be the beginning of World War III.

Revelation 9:16–18 KJV states,

> And the number of the army of horsemen were two hundred thousand thousand: and I heard the number of them.
> And thus I saw the horses in the vision, and them that sat on them, having breastplates of fire,

and of jacinth, and brimstone: and the heads of
the horses were as the heads of lions; and out of
their mouths issued fire and smoke and brimstone [these scriptures describe nuclear weapons
and armies].

By these three was the third part of men
killed, by the fire, and by the smoke, and by the
brimstone, which issued out of their mouths [this
describes nuclear weapons being used to destroy
a third part of the earth].

"And the sixth angel poured out his viral upon the great river
Euphrates; and the water thereof was dried up, that the way of the
kings of the east might be prepared" (Revelation 16:12 KJV). The
east and the north will meet up together at the Euphrates river. This
will definitely start World War III, a global war where all nations will
be involved. Nuclear weapons will hit some parts of the United States
and United Kingdom and the Middle East. Washington, DC, New
York, and several other states will be hit by nuclear weapons.

During the beginning of the tribulation, the Antichrist will
be involved in establishing a peace agreement with Israel and the
Palestinian people. The Antichrist will not be known as the Antichrist
then, he will not let himself be known. "And he shall confirm the
covenant with many for one week: and in the midst of the week
he shall cause the sacrifice and the oblation to cease, and for the
overspreading of abominations he shall make it desolate, even until
the consummation, and that determined shall be poured upon the
desolate" (Daniel 9:27 KJV). Before the abomination of desolation
happens, the third temple at the Temple Mount will be built. After
the third temple is completed, the Jewish people will be allowed to
worship there, and they will perform animal sacrifices, I believe, at
the time.

The Antichrist will reveal himself after three and a half years in
the middle of the seven-year tribulation. But before this happens, the
Bible said in 2 Thessalonians 2:3–4 KJV, "Let no man deceive you by
any means: for that day shall not come, except there come a falling

away first, and that man of sin be revealed the son of perdition. Who opposeth and exalteth himself above all that is called God, or that is worshipped; so that he as God sitteth in the temple of God, showing himself that he is God."

The falling away is people on earth will be so easy to be deceived from the truth of God's magnificent word. (Perdition equals destruction.)

When the antichrist appear during the middle of the tribulation, he will cause the sacrifices to stop. He will be accompanied by the Holy Roman Empire armies. The Antichrist will enter the temple and sit on the throne proclaiming he is God. The Roman armies will attempt to kill and destroy the Jewish people. "And after threescore and two weeks (three years and a half) shall Messiah be cut off, but not for himself: and the people of the prince that shall come shall destroy the city and the sanctuary; and the end thereof shall be with a flood, and unto the end of the war desolations are determined" (Daniel 9:26). The Roman armies will come in the city and slaughter the Jewish people.

Matthew 24:15–21 states,

> When ye therefore shall see the abomination of desolation, spoken of by Daniel the prophet, stand in the holy place (Jerusalem), (whoso readeth, let him understand:)
>
> Then let them which be in Judea flee into the mountains:
>
> Let him which is on the housetop not come down to take anything out of his house:
>
> Neither let him which is in the field return back to take his clothes.
>
> And woe unto them that are unto child, and to them that give suck in those days!
>
> But pray ye that your flight be not in the winter, neither on the sabbath day:

> For then shall be great tribulation, such as
> was not since the beginning of the world to this
> time, no, nor ever shall be.

The Holy Roman armies will come in the city (with fury); they will attack the people of God with so much force no one will have time to get anything, even women who are pregnant will not have time to gather anything for supplies. No one will have time to do anything but flee.

"And when ye shall see Jerusalem compassed with armies, then know that the desolation thereof is nigh" (Luke 21:20 KJV). I will explain at the end of the book why I identify German-led European Union first, then speak about the holy Roman Empire.

"And at that time shall Michael stand up, the great prince which standeth for the children of thy people: and there shall be a time of trouble, such as never was since there was a nation even to that same time: and at that time thy people shall be delivered, every one that shall be found written in the book" (Daniel 12:1 KJV). Many scholars think this is the beginning of the great tribulation, the last 3 and a half years of the tribulation. I don't believe so; I believe the intensity of the tribulation will increase immeasurably. Abomination means "disgust or hatred" (Oxford language dictionary). Desolation means destruction (Oxford language dictionary). The Antichrist hates God's people and will cause destruction to come upon them.

"And to the woman (Israel) were given two wings of a great eagle, that she might fly into the wilderness, into her place, where she is nourished for a time, and times, and half a time, from the face of the serpent (Antichrist). And the serpent cast out of his mouth water as a flood after the woman, that he might cause her to be carried away of the flood" (Revelation 12:14–15).

So God will have a place of safety for his people to go to for three and a half years. The Lord will feed them and keep them from the Antichrist's persecution. There will be some true saints of God where God will keep them from the Antichrist. I believe they are the ones who are not lukewarm. The Antichrist and the Holy Roman Empire will be in the city for forty-two months. "But the court which is without the temple leave out, and measure it not; for it is given unto the Gentiles: and the holy city shall they tread under foot forty and two months" (Revelation 11:2 KJV).

In Revelation 13:1–18 KJV, it explains that the Antichrist will establish a one-world government, a political and military setup. He wants to control the world and kill all God's people. He will run a system to where he convinces the nations he has all the answers to the world's problem. "And I stood upon the sand of the sea, and saw a beast (Antichrist) rise up out of the sea, having seven heads (he will be the seventh head under the Holy Roman Empire/six already came and was destroyed) and ten horns, and upon his horns ten crowns, and upon his heads the name of blasphemy". They will give him great power and great authority.

John saw in a vision that one of the heads was as if it were wounded to death and his deadly wound was healed, and all the world wondered after the beast (Antichrist). He opened his mouth in blasphemy against God attempting to exalt himself over the true, living God. He will make war with the saints (the saints will actually fight the Antichrist and his forces back). He (Antichrist) will overcome them. The Antichrist will control many kindreds and tongues and nations. And all who is on the earth shall worship him whose names are not written in the book of life (eternal life with God). The Antichrist will kill many.

Another beast will come out of the earth, and he will have two horns like a lamb, and he will speak as a dragon. He will appear to be righteous, and he and the Antichrist will work together. The false prophet is who he is, and he will influence people to worship the beast, and he shall do great wonders making fire come down from heaven on the earth in the sight of men. The false prophet will set up a worldwide religion system that will be out of the Holy Roman Empire.

Under the Catholic rules and policies, this empire will force the religion on people on earth; and if they don't follow this religion and the beast (Antichrist), they will be killed. He will deceive many from doing those miracles and convince many to worship the beast as if he were God and those who didn't will be killed. He will cause all—

both small and great, rich and poor, free and bonded—to receive a mark in their right hand or to their foreheads. Receiving the mark means pledging allegiance, loyalty, or commitment of a subordinate to a superior or of an individual to a group or cause. One-world government will consist of no man being able to buy or sell except those who has his mark or the name of the beast or the number of his name. The number of the beast is 666. Read Revelation 13:18. And the dragon was worth(angry) with the woman (church the elect) of God and went to make war with the remnant (small amount of God people) of her seed which keep the commandments of God and have the testimony of Jesus Christ Revelation 12:17 KJV.

Fall of the False Prophet World's False Religion System Revelation Chapter 17 KJV

Judgement will fall on the false religion system of the Holy Roman Empire. Those who believed in this system and committed fornication with her shall experience God's wrath. Verses three to four describe the woman—in this case, the false prophet religion system. Woman in the Bible can stand for a church, Israel, or the false church. The one-world false religion system was very wealthy, very rich. Verse five, "And on her forehead was name written, MYSTERY, BABYLON THE GREAT, THE MOTHER OF HARLOTS AND ABOMINATION OF THE EARTH." A corrupted religion system. In verse six, God called his people (saints) to come out from under her or be killed because of the false prophet religion system. (Martyr equals a person who is killed because of their religious or other beliefs) Oxford Language Dictionary. Verses seven to eight talk about the beast systems that come before this one. In verse nine, the seven heads are seven mountains on which the woman sits (the Holy Roman Empire). Verse eleven states that he will cause destruction upon many. Verse thirteen states that all will have one mind and their power and strength unto the head of the Kings will turn to the beast for help over the politically economic situation. The Roman Empire will rage a war against God and his chosen people who made the resurrection close to the end of the great tribulation. Verses fifteen to eighteen speak of the one-world government system and the one-world false religion system that will be destroyed.

FALL OF THE RELIGIOUS AND ANTICHRIST

Those who are not God's chosen people will not be able to identify that the Antichrist and the false prophet are fakes. They will be totally ignorant of these beasts. They will plead to his rule and policies receiving the Antichrist's number 666. The number will not be tattoo on a person's forehead and right-hand. They will receive God's wrath. The Antichrist will appear to be holy and the false prophet. This appeal will have people believe in his system. The signs and wonders the false prophet do will no doubt confuse many into worshipping the beast because both the Antichrist and false prophet feed off each other.

"Then if any man shall say unto you, Lo, here is Christ, or there; believe it not" (Matthew 24:23 KJV). By studying the word of God every day, a true Christian will not be easily tricked because he or she will know the truth.

FALL OF THE FALSE PROPHET, WORLD RELIGION SYSTEM, AND THE ANTICHRIST

2 Thessalonians 2:1–4 KJV states,

> Now we beseech you, brethren, by the coming of our Lord Jesus Christ, and by our gathering together unto him,
>
> That ye be not upon shaken in mind, or be troubled, neither by spirit, nor by word, nor by letter as from us, as that the day of Christ is at hand (know the truth).
>
> Let no man deceive you by any means: for that day shall not come, except there come a falling away first, and that man of sin be revealed, the son of perdition;
>
> Who opposeth and exalteth himself above all that is called God, or that is worshipped; so that he as God sitteth in the temple of God, showing himself that he is God. The temple will not be in the United States, Great Britain, or any place else but in Jerusalem.

2 Thessalonians 2:8–12 KJV states,

> And then shall that Wicked be revealed, whom the Lord will consume with the spirit of

his mouth, and shall destroy with the brightness of his coming

Even him, whose coming is after the working of Satan with all power and signs and lying wonders,

And with all deceivableness of unrighteousness in them that perish; because they received not the love of the truth, that they might be saved.

And for this cause God shall send them strong delusion, that they should believe a lie:

That they all might be damned who believed not the truth, but had pleasure in unrighteousness.

"Babylon the great has fallen. All nations who have drunk of her wine come out of her, my people, received not her plagues. Her sins have reached heaven. God remembered her iniquities" (Revelation 18:2–5 KJV). The wicked believe in the antichrist agenda and follow it.

"And the beast was taken, and with him the false prophet that wrought miracles before him, with which he deceived them that had received the mark of the beast, and them that worshipped him image. Those both were cast alive into a lake of fire burning with brimstone" (Revelation 19:20 KJV).

SEVEN SEALS, SEVEN TRUMPETS, SEVEN BOWLS

All are pertaining to different times of events that will take place. I have covered four of the seals, false prophet (the Antichrist), the white horse, the red horseman (war), the will be rumors of war (World War III), and the black horseman (famine and starvation). There will be famine, starvation, and there will be a civil war right here in the United States and worldwide because people will do whatever it takes to survive.

Those who will not take the mark of the beast will not be allowed to buy or sell. If you support the beast, the person will suffer God's wrath; and if you don't take the mark, you will die of starvation. Millions will be homeless. The beast will be in control of the food. Many grocery stores and restaurants will be closed because they have no food to sell. The world will be in so much distress, it will be a panic nationwide. This will be a terrible, horrifying time here on earth. God will keep the faithful who belong to him, he will provide for them. With the pale horseman, a fourth part of the earth will be killed by sword—hunger and death will happen. Pestilence will happen because if people cannot or don't have food, they will get some type of disease. The reader needs to study the Books of Revelation chapters 5–8 KJV. All these chapters will explain it in further details.

The seven trumpets will take place during the great tribulation. Revelation chapter 9 speaks about World War III. Nuclear weapons will hit some parts of the United States (New York, Washington, DC, probably Los Angeles, and Chicago), and other places will be affected by nuclear weapons. London will be hit by a nuclear blast. Major earth disasters will happen. Revelation chapter 11 tells of Jesus's second coming and more.

The seven bowls/vial judgments are the last judgments of the tribulation at the near end of it. Revelation chapter 16 talks about the seven bowls. Under God's wrath, for instance, sores may come on people's body who had the mark of the beast. The plague is mainly attacking those who support the Antichrist. The sea turns into blood, and every living creature in the sea dies.

In Revelation 16:8–9 KJV, the sun will become so hot that it will torment the people on earth. Even the Antichrist will have a chance to repent of the evil he will do, but he will refuse to do so. Armies will gather at the place of Armageddon. They (armies) will get ready to fight each other but sees Jesus Christ coming with his angels and resurrected saints. All of the armies will fight Christ instead. Islands will be moved; mountains will not be found; hailstones will fall on mankind. They will blaspheme God because of the plague of hail. I believe the hail that fall from the sky will weigh between 100 to 150 pounds. Jerusalem will experience a major earthquake like never before. It will split into three parts. In Revelation chapter 17 KJV, God will take vengeance out on those people because of the blood of the prophets and His holy people who were slaughtered here on earth. In Revelation chapter 18, the world will cry about the fall of Babylon. Verse 8 describes she will be destroyed.

Armageddon Second Coming of Jesus Christ and the Millennium

"And he shall send his angels with a great sound of a trumpet, and they shall gather together his elect (saints that are alive and the saints who died years ago) from the four winds, from one end of heaven to the other (Jesus spoke of this)" (Matthew 24:31 KJV).

1 Thessalonians 4:15–17 states,

> For this we say unto you by the word of the Lord, that we which are alive and remain unto the coming of the Lord shall not prevent them which are asleep.
>
> For the Lord himself shall descend from heaven with a shout, with the voice of the archangel, and with the trump of God: and the dead in Christ shall rise first:
>
> Then we which are alive and remain shall be caught up together with them in the clouds, to meet the Lord in the air: and so shall we ever be with the Lord.

"Now this I say, brethren, that flesh and blood cannot inherit the kingdom of God; neither doth corruption inherit incorruption" (1 Corinthians 15:50 KJV).

"In a moment, in the twinkling of an eye, at the last trump: for the trumpet shall sound, and the dead shall be raised incorruptible, and we shall be changed" (1 Corinthians 15:52 KJV).

This fleshly body cannot enter the kingdom of God. We have to have a spiritual body. A person has to be born again, the Holy Spirit will dwell in them. That is what is going back to heaven—your spiritual body.

"And the seventh angel sounded; and there were voices in heaven, saying, The kingdoms of this world are become the kingdoms of our Lord, and of his Christ; and he shall reign forever and ever" Revelation 11:15 KJV.

"And I saw the beast, and the kings of the earth, and their armies, gathered together to make war against him (Christ) that sat on the horse, and against his army. And the beast was taken, and with him the false prophet that wrought miracles before him, with which he deceived them that had received the mark of the beast, and them that worshipped his image (statute or a robot) the mark of the beast is not keeping the true sabbath which is Saturday. The antichrist will make it mandatory for all to worship him on Sunday. These both were cast alive into a lake of fire burning with brimstone" (Revelation 19:19–20 KJV).

Zechariah 14:1–5 KJV states,

> Behold the day of the Lord cometh and the spoil shall be divided in the midst of thee.
>
> For I will gather all nations against Jerusalem to battle: and the city shall be taken and the houses rifled and the women ravished and half of the city shall go forth into captivity and the residue of the people shall not be cut off from the city.
>
> Then shall the Lord go forth and fight against those nations as when he fought in the day of battle.
>
> And his feet shall stand in that day upon the Mount of Olives, which is before Jerusalem on

the east, and the Mount of Olives shall remove toward the north and half of it toward the south.

And ye shall flee to the valley of the mountain shall reach unto Azal, yea, ye shall flee like as ye fled from before the earthquake in the days of Uzziah, King of Judea and the Lord my God shall come, and all the saints with thee.

Jerusalem will be surrounded and attacked by the armies—the city will be under siege. Just when it looks like Jerusalem was about to lose the fight, Jesus Christ shows up with His army (saints and His angels). He will punish the opposing force.

"And the armies which were in heaven followed him upon white horses, clothed in fine linen, white and clean" (Revelation 19:14 KJV).

"And in the days of these kings shall the God of heaven set up a kingdom, which shall never be destroyed: and the kingdom shall not be left to other people, but it shall break in pieces and consume all these kingdoms, and it shall stand forever" (Daniel 2:44 KJV).

"I beheld till the thrones were cast down, and the Ancient of days did sit, whose garment was white as snow, and the hair of his head like the pure wool: his throne was like the fiery flame, and his wheels as burning fire" (Daniel 7:9 KJV).

This will take place in the latter days at the end of the age. Daniel 7:11–14 KJV states,

I beheld then because of the voice of the great words which the horn spake: I beheld even till the beast was slain, and his body destroyed, and given to the burning flame.

As concerning the rest of the beasts, they had their dominion taken away; yet their lives were prolonged for a season and time.

I saw in the night visions, and, behold, one like the Son of man came with the clouds of heaven, and came to the Ancient of days, and they brought him near before him.

And there was given him dominion, and glory, and a kingdom, that all people, nations, and languages, should serve him: his dominion is an everlasting dominion, which shall not pass away, and his kingdom that which shall not be destroyed.

All through the Bible, it speaks about Jesus returning (second coming). God said to study to be approved by God. "Study to show thyself approved unto God, a workman that needeth not to be ashamed, rightly dividing the word of truth" (2 Timothy 2:15 KJV).

Behold, I come as a thief. Blessed is he that watcheth and keepth his garments, lest he walk naked and they see his shame (serve the Lord and not give up).

And he gathered them together into a place called in the Hebrew tongue Armageddon (Revelation 16:15).

Zephaniah 1:14–18 KJV states,

The great day of the Lord is near, It is near and hasteth greatly, even the voice of the day of the Lord the mighty man shall cry there bitterly.

That day is a day of wrath, a day of trouble and distress, a day of wasteness and desolation, a day of darkness and gloominess, a day of clouds and thick darkness.

A day of trumpet and alarm against the fenced cities, and against the high towers.

And I will bring distress upon men, that they shall walk like blind men, because they have

> sinned against the LORD: and their blood shall be poured out as dust, and their flesh as the dung.
>
> Neither their silver nor their gold shall be able to deliver them in the day of the LORD's wrath; but the whole land shall be devoured by the fire of his jealousy: for he shall make even a speedy riddance of them that dwell in the land.

"I will also gather all nations, and will bring them down into the valley of Jehoshaphat, and will plead with them there for my people and for my heritage Israel, whom they have scattered among the nations, and parted my hand" (Joel 3:2 KJV). So the devil will gather all the nations at Armageddon. Antichrist and the European armies, which is the Holy Roman Empire, will battle the nation of Israel. They will be redirected (by Jesus Christ) to the east of Jerusalem to the Valley of Jehoshaphat between the city of the Mount of Olives. "Where the Lord will smite all the people that have fought against Jerusalem. Their flesh will be consumed away, their eyes, mouth and tongue will be consumed" (Zechariah 14:12 KJV). "Blow ye the trumpet of Zion, and sound an alarm in my holy mountain: let all the inhabitants of the land tremble: for the day of the LORD cometh, for it is nigh at hand. A day of darkness and of gloominess, a day of clouds and of thick darkness, as the morning spread upon the mountains: a great people and a strong; there hath not been over the like, neither shall be any more after it, even to the years of many generations" (Joel 2:1–2 KJV). "Before their face the people shall be much pained: all faces shall gather blackness" (Joel 2:6). "The earth shall quake before them; the heavens shall tremble: the sun and the moon shall be dark, and the stars shall withdraw their shining" (Joel 2:10). Nuclear weapons will be used in this conflict. I also believe the Asian armies will be involved in this war, but I believe Jesus will let some of them return to their homeland. Jesus Christ will let some go in this battle, but the next one after the thousand year is up, when Israel dwells in peace, Jesus Christ will destroy them all. "After many days thou shalt be visited: in the latter years thou shalt come into the land that is brought back from the sword, and is gathered out of many people, against the mountains of Israel, which have been always waste: but it is brought forth out of the nations, and they shall dwell safely all of them" (Ezekiel 38:8).

Ezekiel 38:14–16 states,

> Therefore, son of man, prophesy and say unto Gog, Thus saith the Lord GOD; In that day when my people of Israel dwelleth safely, shalt thou not know it?
>
> And thou shalt come from thy place out of the north parts, thou, and many people with thee, all of the riding upon horses, a great company, and a mighty army:
>
> And though shalt come up against my people Israel, as a cloud to cover the land; it shall be in the latter days, and I will bring thee against my land, that the heathen may know me, when I shall be sanctified in thee, O Gog, before their eyes.

"And I will send a fire on Magog, and among them that dwell carelessly in the isles: and they shall know that I am the LORD" (Ezekiel 39:6). After these major events, then comes the millennium. No, the earth will not be destroyed then, there will still be people on earth. Jesus Christ will set up His kingdom on earth for a thousand years to teach man how to live in peace.

"And he laid hold on the dragon, that old serpent, which is the Devil and Satan and bound (prison) him a thousand years" (Revelation 20:2 KJV).

"And Jesus said unto them, Verily I say unto you, That ye which have followed me, in the regeneration when the Son of man shall sit in the throne of his glory, ye also shall sit upon twelve thrones, judging the twelve tribes of Israel" (Matthew 19:28 KJV).

"And I saw thrones, and they sat upon them, and judgement was given unto them: and I saw the souls of them that were beheaded for the witness of Jesus and for the word of God and which had not worshipped the beast, neither his image, neither had received his mark upon their foreheads or in their hands; and they lived and reigned with Christ a thousand years" (Revelation 20:4 KJV).

These are the ones who was resurrected back to life.

"Blessed and holy is he that hath part in the first resurrection: on such the second death hath no power, but they shall be priests of God and of Christ, and shall reign with him a thousand years" (Revelation 20:6 KJV).

We'll have work to do during the thousand years, teaching the nations of the world how to live in peace.

THE MILLENNIUM

The two witnesses will be killed near the end of the sixth trumpet sounded. God will ascend them to heaven. Revelation 11:11-14 KJV. The resurrection for the saints of God will happen on the seventh trumpet sound where the dead and alive in Christ shall ascend to heaven.

Isaiah 2:2–4 KJV states,

> And it shall come to pass in the last days, that the mountain of the LORD's house shall be established in the top of the mountains, and shall be exalted above the hills; and all nations shall flow unto it.
>
> And many people shall go and say, Come ye, and let us go up to the mountain of the LORD, to the house of the God of Jacob; and he will teach us of his ways, and we will walk in his paths: for out of Zion shall go forth the law, and the word of the LORD from Jerusalem.
>
> And he shall judge among the nations, and shall rebuke many people: and they beat their swords into plowshares, and their spears into pruninghooks: nation shall not lift up sword against nation, neither shall they learn war any more.

Jesus will set a standard of His laws. Jesus will also judge between the nations and will settle international disputes. They will not learn war among them anymore.

"And it shall come to pass, that every one that is left of all the nations which came against Jerusalem shall even go up from year to year to worship the King, the LORD of hosts, and to keep the feast of tabernacles. And it shall be, that whoso will not come up of all the families of the earth unto Jerusalem to worship the King, the LORD of hosts, even upon them shall be no rain" (Zechariah 14:16–17 KJV). God will cut them off until they become submissive.

After the Millennium Gog and Magog

Revelation 20:7–9 KJV states,

> And when the thousand years are expired, Satan shall be loosed out of prison,
>
> And shall go out to deceive the nations which are in the four quarters of the earth, Gog, and Magog, to gather them together to battle: the number of whom is the sand of the sea.
>
> And they went up on the breadth of the earth, and compassed the camp of the saints about, and the beloved city: and fire came down from God out of heaven, and devoured them.

Who is Gog and Magog and their allies that will come with them? Later on in my life studying on this subject, books I read and listened to several preachers on this matter, all of them said that Gog is the ruler of Russia and the country of Russia and Magog is the country of Russia. Well, from extensive study, I found out part of this is not true. Gog is the ruler of Russia, but Magog is the country of China, not the country of Russia. (Read the history on the descendants of Magog.)

"Son of man, set thy face against Gog, the land of Magog, the chief prince of Meshech and Tubal, and prophesy against him" (Ezekiel 38:2 KJV). The region of Meshach is often identified as north of the Black Sea, southern Russia and Ukraine, and possibly Republic of Georgia. Tubal is an area in central Turkey.

Ezekiel 38:3–5 KJV states,

> And say, Thus saith the Lord GOD; Behold,
> I am against thee, O Gog, the chief prince of
> Meshech and Tubal. (Russia ruler is prince over
> these territories [Gotquestion.org].)
> And I will turn thee back, and put hooks
> unto thy jaws, and I will bring thee forth, and
> all thine army, horses and horsemen, all of them
> clothed with all sorts of armour, even a great
> company with bucklers and shields, all of them
> handling swords.
> Persia, Ethiopia, and Libya with them; all of
> them with shield and helmet.

Persia is the country of Iran, Libya, Ethiopia, and (northeast Africa) Sudan.

"Gomer, and all his bands; the house of Togarmah of the north quarters, and all his bands: and many people with thee" (Ezekiel 38:6 KJV).

"After many days, thou shall be visited: in the latter years thou shalt come into the land that is brought back from the sword, and is gathered out of many people, against the mountain of Israel, which have been always waste: but it is brought forth out of the nations, and they shall dwell safely all of them" (Ezekiel 38:8 KJV). Some biblical scholars say that Russia and her allies will attack Israel and that will be the beginning of World War III but I found out this is an honest mistake. If a person would read the book of Revelation chapter 20 and study it very carefully with other references books (history), Gog (Russia ruler/Magog China) will attack Israel after the millennium when Israel is in peace.

Ezekiel 38:10–12 states,

> Thus saith the Lord God; It shall also come
> to pass, that at the same time shall things come

into thy mind, and thou shalt think an evil thought:

And thou shall say, I will go up to the land of unwalled villages; I will go to them that are at rest, that dwell safely, all of them dwelling without walls, and having neither bars nor gates,

To take spoil, and to take a prey; to turn them hand upon the desolate places that are now inhabited, and upon the people that are gathered out of the nations, which have gotten cattle and goods, that dwell in the midst of the land.

Yes, God has blessed the country of Israel with many resources. This country is no bigger than the state of New Jersey or possibly Annapolis, Maryland, but God has blessed Israel above measure. You will think as many wars this country has been in, it would be a land of poverty, but Israel is God's chosen people. If a person would read the Old Testament, it's very evident that God continually blessed this country because of the covenant He made with Abraham, Isaac, and Jacob. Genesis 12:3, 7; Genesis 17:4, 7–8, and Genesis 22:17 explained in detail why He blessed Abraham and check Genesis 17:26 and Genesis chapter 28.

"Therefore, son of man, prophesy and say unto Gog, Thus saith the Lord GOD; In that day when my people of Israel dwelleth safely, shalt thou not know it? And thou shalt come from thy place out of the north parts, thou, and many people with thee, all of them riding upon horses, a great company, and a mighty army" (Ezekiel 38:14–15 KJV).

"And it shall come to pass at the same time when Gog shall come against the land of Israel, saith the Lord GOD, that my fury shall come up in my face" (Ezekiel 38:18 KJV).

"And I will plead against him with pestilence and with blood; and I will rain upon him, and upon his bands, and upon the many people that are with him, an overflowing rain, and great hailstones, fire, and brimstone" (Ezekiel 38:22 KJV).

These events will happen around the time Jesus Christ fight the Antichrist armies and other armies in the valley of Jehoshaphat. Revelation 14: 19–20 states; And the angel thrust in his sickle into the earth, and gathered the vine of the earth, and cast it into the great winepress of the wrath of God. And the winepress was trodden without the city, and blood came out of the winepress, even unto the horse bridle, by the space of a thousand and six hundred furlongs. Yes, the blood from the soldiers will be four feet high and the blood will reach 200 miles long I believe. Revelation 14:19-20 will happen at the time of the nations gathered at Armageddon. But when Israel is in peace after the millennium God will destroy all the nations that attack them which will be Russia and China and their allies.

New Heaven and New Earth

Revelation stands for revealing the future after the destruction of Russia's leader and his allies.

"And the devil that deceived them was cast unto the lake of fire and brimstone, where the beast and his false prophets are, and shall be tormented day and night forever and ever" (Revelation 20:10 KJV).

"But the day of the Lord will come as a thief in the night; in the which the heavens shall pass away with a great noise, and the elements shall melt with fervent heat, the earth also and the works that are therein shall be burned up" (2 Peter 3:10 KJV).

Revelation 21:1–5 KJV states,

> And I saw a new heaven and a new earth: for the first heaven and the first earth were passed away; and there was no more sea.
>
> And I John saw the holy city, new Jerusalem, coming down from God out of heaven, prepared as a bride adorned for her husband.
>
> And I heard a great voice out of heaven saying, Behold, the tabernacle of God is with men, and he will dwell with them, and they shall be his people, and God himself shall be with them, and be their God.
>
> And God shall wipe away all tears from their eyes; and there shall be no more death, neither sorrow, nor crying, neither shall there be any more pain: for the former things are passed away.

> And he that sat upon the throne said,
> Behold, I make all things new. And he said unto
> me, Write: for these words are true and faithful.

Revelation 21:10–22 KJV talk about what heaven and earth look like. In verse 23, the city needs neither sun nor moon to shine. The glory of God did lighten it. Verse 24 states, "And the nations of them which are saved shall walk in the light of it: and the kings of the earth do bring their glory and honor into it."

Revelation chapter 22 basically talks about the saints are busy serving God Almighty for eternity and also reigns with Jesus Christ. Imagine being with God for eternity. This will be unbelievable, amazing, and brings great joy. In John 14:2 KJV, Jesus said, "In my Father's house are many mansions: if it were not so, I would have told you. I go to prepare a place for you." The mansions that are here on earth now will be no comparison to the mansions in heaven (unreal). "But as it is written, Eye hath not seen, nor ear heard, neither have entered into the heart of man, the things which God hath prepared for them that love him" 1 Corinthians 2:9 KJV. This Scripture, I believe, is talking about the present and the future of blessings. What a wonderful Almighty God we serve! "Blessed are they that do his commandments, that they may have rights to the tree of life, and may enter in through the gates into the city" Revelation 22:14 KJV. You see, God has a master plan for those who love him here on earth and the future new heaven and earth.

Two Witnesses

Revelation chapter 11 speaks about the two witnesses will be human beings not spiritual beings.

"And there was given me a reed like a rod: and the angel stood, saying, Rise, and measure the temple of God, and the altar, and them that worship therein. But the court which is without the temple leave out, and measure it not; for it is given unto the Gentiles: and the holy city shall they tread under foot forty and two months (three years and a half)" Revelation 11:1–2 KJV.

Verse 1 explains God's temple is the church of God who are His true Christian followers of Christ. Verse 2 explains, I believe, those in the temple who worship God. As far as the trampled underfoot, I believe it means John, in his vision, saw the true church, but the church was trampled underfoot by those who is the true church but have the spirit of the false Antichrist.

"And I will give you power unto my two witnesses, and they shall prophesy a thousand two hundred and threescore days, clothed in sackcloth (three and a half years). These are the two olive trees, and the two candlesticks standing before the God of the earth" Revelation 11:3–4 KJV.

Some scholars (most) say these two witnesses are Moses and Elijah or Moses and Enoch, I believe. It could be in the days of Moses and Elijah, they did mighty miracles during their day when they were alive. Some scholars say that God will bring Moses and Elijah back to life to perform miracles in the midst of the people on earth to prove God is real and to have men on earth accept Jesus Christ as their Savior. All this will begin at the last three and a half years of the tribulation. The two witnesses will be human beings not spiritual beings. They will have God power like Moses and Elijah had in the ancient Bible days.

"And if any man will hurt them, fire proceedeth out of their mouth, and devoureth their enemies: and if any man will hurt them, he must in this manner be killed" Revelation 11:5 KJV.

In verse 3, the sackcloth represents sorrow for sin, lampstands, the light of the world, representing the Lord. The olive trees represent a double-anointing on the two witnesses. The two witnesses will have the power to kill those who oppose them. In verse 6, these two witnesses will have power to shut heaven that it rain not in the days of their prophecy and will have power over waters to turn them to blood and to smite the earth with all plagues as often as they will just like in the days of Moses and Elijah. See the books of Exodus and 1 Kings, it spoke about the miracles both performed in those days.

"And when they shall have finished their testimony, the beast that ascendeth out of the bottomless pit shall make war against them, and shall overcome them, and kill them" Revelation 11:7 KJV.

The bottomless pit refers to a holding place for the disobedient, a Greek word also uses translated abyss, angels that followed Satan. This person that will attack the two witnesses is the Antichrist and his allies. They will fight one another until the Antichrist will kill them. It will be an all-out war among them.

"And their dead bodies shall lie in the street of the great city (Jerusalem), which spiritually is called Sodom and Egypt, where also our Lord was crucified. And they of the people and kindreds and tongues and nations shall see their dead bodies three days and an half, and shall not suffer their dead bodies to be put in graves" Revelation 11:8–9.

And "people and kindreds and tongues and nations shall see their dead bodies" let me knows that people will probably see this nationwide on television, or some other way. People will, it seems to me, hate the two witnesses so much that they will not bother to bury the two witnesses. They will leave them in the streets for people to view their bodies.

Revelation 11:10–12 KJV states,

And they that dwell upon the earth shall rejoice over them, and make merry, and shall send gifts one to another; because these two prophets tormented them that dwelt on the earth. (People will actually celebrate that they are finally dead.)

And after three days and an half the spirit of life from God entered into them, and they stood upon their feet; and great fear fell upon them which saw them.

And they heard a great voice from heaven saying unto them, Come up hither. And they ascended up to heaven in a cloud; and their enemies beheld them.

THE BOOK OF REVELATION

Revelation chapter 7 talks about those who are sealed from tribes of Israel—144,000—in the great tribulation. They will be protected in the tribulation because they will have a mission to perform during this time. They will tell everyone of Jesus Christ's salvation.

"After this I beheld, and lo, a great multitude, which no man could number, of all nations, and kindreds, and people, and tongues, stood before the throne, and before the Lamb, clothed with white robes, and palms in their hands" Revelation 7:9 KJV.

THE TRUTH ABOUT GOD'S PROPHECIES

All throughout history man has rebelled against the almighty God. God's word has specific instructions, standards, commandments, and laws to follow. Man does not believe in God's word (Holy Scriptures) that includes His prophecies.

You see, God wants us to be blessed, and the way to be blessed is to obey His commandments. But when we continually refuse to obey Him, He will send a prophet to warn us of the disaster that will happen if we do not turn away from sin. Man did things their own way trying to establish peace among nations but has failed miserably. As we look at the world today, war is going on in certain countries, and in some places, famines are happening in some countries because of their sins and iniquities. In the United States. racism is on the rampage, riots seem to be everywhere, and murder is at an all-time high in several cities. When will these things stop? It won't. Man is disobedience to God's commandments and His laws.

In the book of Matthew 24:3–8, Jesus spoke of the end of the age.

> And as he sat upon the mount of Olives the disciples came unto him privately saying, Tell us when shall these things be? And what shall be the sign of thy coming and of the end of the world? And Jesus answered and said unto them. Take heed that no man deceives you. For many shall come in my name saying, I am Christ and shall deceive many. This verse is basically saying

many will say I follow Christ and they know the true way to salvation but they are false prophets deceiving many that this is the true way to Christ (teaching a different gospel). And he shall hear of wars and rumors of wars: see that ye be not troubled: (afraid) for all these things must come to pass, but the end is not yet. For nation shall rise against nation and kingdom against kingdom and there shall be famine and pestilences, and earthquakes in diver places. All these are the beginning of sorrows (grief).

Looking at the world today. There is a threat from several countries of using nuclear weapons on them. Countries always want to dominate other countries, the reason being lust—that the bottom line is they want more territory in their possession; as you can see, oil and gas have become a big subject in most countries. The world has gone mad, sinning against God worst and worst. 2 Peter 3:3–4 states,

> Knowing this first that there shall come in the last day's scoffers, walking after their own lusts.
>
> And saying, "Where is the promise of his coming? For since the Fathers fell asleep all things continue as they were from the beginning of the creation."

Jesus Christ stated in Matthews 24:21, "For then shall be great tribulation such as was not since the beginning of the world to this time no, nor ever shall be." This, my brother and sister, speaks about a nuclear blast. In verse 22, Jesus stated, "Except those days should be shortened, there should no flesh be saved, but for the elect's sake those days shall be shortened." Yes, because of Gods' true servants. He will return to earth (Jesus Christ) and stop this madness. The lukewarm Christians who do not serve God with a whole heart will be in the Great Tribulation. The main reason why Jesus Christ hasn't returned yet is that it's not time yet—but make no mistake about it; it will be in the near future.

But there will come a time that this long-suffering of man will come to a stop. Revelation 10:6 states,

> And swore by him that liveth for ever and ever who created, however, and the things that therein are and the earth and the things which are therein, that there should be time no longer: It will be a time of no more delay.

There will be a time when the country Germany and the Holy Roman Empire will attack the previous countries I discussed to be an attack with nuclear weapons. The beast (Antichrist), which is Germany leader, and the false prophet will be revealed. The Antichrist will run the military and political part, and the false prophet will run the religious system in Europe and, eventually, the whole world.

Proof of Nuclear Blast

Ezekiel 6:6 states,

> In all your dwelling places the cities shall be laid waste and the high places shall be desolate: that your altars may be laid waste and made desolate, and your idols may be broken and cease; and your images, may be cut down and your works, maybe abolished.

God is going to use Germany and the Holy Roman Empire, and then later He will destroy the nation of Germany and the Holy Roman Empire.

The book of Amos chapter 5 verse 3 talks about the effect of a nuclear blast. "For thus saith the Lord God; The city that went out by a thousand shall have a hundred, and that which went forth by a hundred shall leave ten to the house of Israel." This is clearly talking about the results of a nuclear weapon. It also clearly talks about what will happen from the radiation of a nuclear blast. The word *Israel* in this verse is talking about the United States, Great Britain, and Judah. It is not the country of Israel. Read and study your Bible on the prophecy of the United States and Great Britain in the book of Genesis.

> And it shall come to pass of there remain ten men in one house, that they shall die. And a man's uncle shall take him up and be that burneth him to bring out the bones out of the house, and shall say unto him that is by the sides of the

house. Is there yet any with thee? And he shall say no. Then shall he say Hold thy tongue for we may not make mention of the name of the Lord. Amos 6:9–10

This is self-explanatory. Jesus Christ will keep His people from the hour of destruction.

> Because thou hast kept the word of my patience, I also will keep thee from the hour of temptation which shall come upon all the world, to try them that dwell upon the earth. Revelation 3:10

> And to the woman (church) were given two wings of a great eagle (escape) that she might fly into the wilderness into her place where she is nourished for a time and times and half a time from the face of the serpent. Revelation 12:14

You got to know that the Bible speaks in symbols; *time* means basically one year, *times* is two years, and *half of the time* is six months, so Jesus Christ will put His people (Christians) in a place of safety and take care of them providing everything they need supernaturally. But before these things will happen, we as God's people must wear out the wicked.

> When I say unto the wicked. Thou shalt surely die and thou givest him not warning, nor speakest to warn the wicked from his wicked way; to save his life: the same wicked man shall die in his iniquity: but his blood will I require at thine hand. Ezekiel 3:18

Being a Christian, you know what's about to happen in prophecies in the Bible, and don't tell anyone and that person dies not hearing the warning message from God's word; that person who is a Christian will be punished.

Ezekiel chapter 33:8 states, "When I say until the wicked I wicked man thou shall surely die, if thou dost not speak to warn the wicked from his way that wicked man shall die in his iniquity but his blood will I require at thine hand." Right now as I am writing this book, I will discuss Revelation 9:14–20 where it talks about the sixth angel (seal) loosen the four angels, in which one was bound in the great Euphrates River. An army of two hundred million will go across to battle in World War III: the river is dried up at this time when this occurs. (Right now, the river is drying up.)

It explains in verse 18, a third of men will be killed by tanks, aircraft, and other military weapons.

> And the sixth angel poured out his vial upon
> the great river Euphrates and the water thereof
> was dried up that the way of the kings of the east
> might be prepared. Revelation 16:12

World War III will lead to the final battle of all the armies, who will gather at Armageddon. Jesus Christ will return with His army His saints.

> I will gather all the nations and bring them
> down into the valley of Jehoshaphat and will
> plead with them there for my people and for
> my heritage Israel (country Israel) whom they
> have scattered among the nations and parted my
> Land. Joel 3:2

God does not want anyone to perish. In Acts 2:38, it states,

> Then Peter said unto them. "Repent and
> be baptized every one of you in the name of
> Jesus Christ for the remission of sins and ye shall
> receive the gift of the Holy Spirit."

God wants everyone to have salvation; He is loving, compassionate, and merciful. He doesn't want to see anybody perish. In the book of John 3:16, it says,

> For God so loved the world, that he gave
> his only begotten Son that whosoever believeth in
> him should not perish, but have everlasting life.

Isn't this wonderful? Jesus Christ wants you and me to live with Him in the millennium and for eternal, so please, brother and sister, give your life to Christ. You will never regret it. In the natural realm, we will not live forever. One day we have to give account for wrong and right doings in the judgment seat.

> Jesus stated, "Then shall he say also unto
> them on the left hand, Depart from ye cursed
> into everlasting fire prepared for the devil and his
> angels." Matthew 25:41

What are you going to do then? Nothing—it will be too late then. So please, sir and ma'am, give your life to Christ to serve Him, obey Him, and keep His commandments. Only those who keep His commandments shall make it into the Kingdom of God.

Important Revelation Scriptures

1) Matthew 24:4—Many will come in Jesus's name and say they are the Christ and deceive many.
2) 1 John 2:18—This is the last hour as you heard that the Antichrist is coming, many Antichrist have come. This is the last hour (near the end of age).
3) 1 John 2:22—Who is a liar? He denies that Jesus is the Christ; Antichrist denies the Father and the Son.
4) Matthew 24:24—False Christs and false prophets will perform great signs and wonders, if possible, to lead astray the elect (saints).
5) Daniel 11:21—He shall come without warning and obtain the kingdom by flatteries (Antichrist).
6) 1 John 4:1—Don't believe every spirit, but test the spirit to see if the person is of God. Many false prophets have come.
7) 1 John 4:2–3—Every spirit that does not confess Jesus is not from God, this is the spirit of the Antichrist you heard that come. He is already in the world. Every spirit (man) confesses Jesus Christ came in the flesh is from God.
8) Daniel 7:24—Ten horns out of this kingdom are the ten kings but another will arise after them. He shall subdue three kings. That king will be Jesus Christ and His saints.
9) Daniel 11:36—The Antichrist will do what he wishes, he will exalt himself and magnify himself; he will speak astonishing things (very intelligent/knowing everything). He will prosper in all he does.

10) Daniel 8:25—With his policies, he shall cause craft to prosper and shall magnify himself in his heart. He shall destroy many (lukewarm Christians/many who will not take his mark and worship the image). He will stand up against the Prince of princes, Jesus Christ. (But Jesus Christ shall, at the end, throw him in the lake of fire with the false prophet.)

11) Revelation 20:10—The devil who deceived them was thrown in the lake of fire with the beast and false prophet. They continually will be tormented forever and ever.

12) Mark 13:9—Jesus said many will deliver you up to councils, and in the synagogues, you will be beaten and taken to kings and rulers in the last days for a testimony against them.

13) Revelation 13:15—The Antichrist has power to give life (breath) to the image of the beast (possibly a robot); he should speak that as many would not worship the image of the beast, they should be killed. This can be also the false prophet able to perform false miracles to deceive many people on earth. Or the false prophet is able to give the image (robot) the ability to speak or have a statue to worship the Antichrist image. The robots may be added to his plan.

Important Notes At the Beginning of the Great Tribulation and After

At the beginning of the Great Tribulation, the Antichrist will assist with establishing a peace treaty with Israel and the Palestinian people. At the end of the first three and a half years of the Great Tribulation, the Antichrist will break the peace treaty. The Jewish people, I believe, will be doing animal sacrifices at the third temple that will be built before this incident happens. This is the abomination of desolation where the Antichrist (Germany) and the Holy Roman empire will attack the Jewish people in Judea, and they will have to flee to the mountains. The Antichrist will enter the temple and sit on the throne, proclaiming he is God. The king of the South—Iran—and his Muslim allies attack the king of the North—Germany—and his armies, and the North will defeat them. China and Russia will attack the North, Germany, and their armies and defeat them. World War 3 will start. United States will be hit with nuclear weapons; Great Britain and other nations will be hit with nuclear weapons. Revelation 9:13–18 states that four angels were bound to be released at the great Euphrates River that will dry up. Two hundred million soldiers from the East will enter the Euphrates River—China and Russia, I believe. The great Euphrates River begins, I believe, with the country Turkey and down through Syria and Iraq and finish at the Persian Gulf. This is the area where World War 3 will start. A third of mankind will be killed by nuclear weapons and, like I stated, will hit some parts of the United States and other nations.

1) The two witnesses will be resurrected at the end of the sixth trumpet.
2) The true saints dead and alive will be resurrected blowing of the seventh trumpet.
3) Armies will gather at Armageddon (Megiddo) at the lower Galilee region of northern Israel. I believe this will be a regional war where the Antichrist and his armies, those that follow him, will go to battle against Jesus Christ, and the army of God will show up just when it may seem Israel may lose this battle. All of the armies will turn and fight Jesus Christ and his army, the battle will end up at the valley of Jehoshaphat. Jesus Christ will prevail them and thrown the Antichrist and the false prophet in the lake of fire.
4) The saints will reign with Jesus Christ for a thousand years in Jerusalem. The devil will be thrown in prison for a thousand years. At the expire of the thousand years, he will be released from prison where he will deceive the nations again. During the thousand years, Jesus Christ will teach nations how to live in peace. Some saints will be kings and priests of the twelve tribes of Israel.
5) After a thousand years, Satan will be released from prison where he will deceive the nations.
6) Russia, China, and their allies will attack Israel because during this time they will be dwelling in the land of peace (nation of Israel).
7) Jesus Christ will defend for Israel and destroy all the armies.
8) Satan will be thrown in the lake of fire for eternity.
9) White-throne judgement will take place and the final judgement.
10) The old heaven and earth will be destroyed by fire.
11) New heaven and earth where the saints will live with Christ forever.

"And I saw three unclean spirits like frogs come out of the mouth of the dragon, and out of the mouth of the beast, and out of the mouth of the false prophet" Revelation 16:13 KJV. The beast and the false prophet were controlled by Satan.

Revelation 13:4 KJV states, "And they worshipped the dragon (devil) which gave power unto the beast: and they worshipped the beast, saying, Who is like unto the beast? Who is able make war with him?"

First, the European Union will have a twenty-eight-nation unity; but in the European Union led by Germany, some nations will depart from under the European Union down to a ten-nation confederacy in the last days. If a person will search the Scriptures in the Bible and read history books on Germany (ancient history), Germany, with the Roman empire started major wars especially World Wars I and II. By reading the Holy Bible, it indicates they were warriors. The German military government involves the Catholic Church for political gain and more. In the Bible, names like Assyrian and Assur represent today's Germany. By reading history on these people from the beginning, their intention was to take over the world and still is. After World War II, Germany basically went undercover (underground). No one is really paying attention to the country of Germany, but they are still getting ready to take over the world, building there military backup. They will be in power again. Germany, right now, is the leading nation in Europe.

Germany will violate foreign policy. Germany will try and take over Europe and Middle East also. It will be an oil conflict that will have Iran and their allies attack them. Daniel 11:40 explains this. The south (Iran and their allies) attacks the north Germany—European Union. The European Union will defeat them. But as I explained in the beginning of the book, China and Russia will see this and attack the north and destroy them causing World War III to happen. I believe Germany will join forces with Russia and China to fight Jesus Christ with his armies after a thousand years. Jesus will destroy them with rain and great hailstones, fire, and brimstones. God will destroy these demonic forces and establish His kingdom that will last forever. *Hallelujah*!

"And I saw the beast, and the kings of the earth, and their armies, gathered together to make war against him that sat on the horse, and against his army" Revelation 19:19.

God will win at the end and His people. Conditions will really get very bad, and it will be a very difficult time to survive during the great tribulation. I must say Christians believe they will be raptured before the great tribulation begins. By reading and studying your Bible, there's no evidence of a pre-rapture taking place. John Nelson Darby (1800s) started this illusion about the rapture taking place during the last days before the tribulation. So many movies were made on the rapture with producers making millions. Preachers are misleading their congregations (not all but majority of them). This is actually what happens when people don't totally realize the wisdom and understanding from God— a huge misinterpretation.

But if a person will thoroughly read Matthew chapter 24 very carefully, Jesus Christ's second coming will be after the tribulation. No man knows the day nor the hour, not even the angels in heaven. Matthew chapter 24 do give you a season that it is close. Revelation 19:14 indicates clearly that Jesus's second coming will happen just around the time Armageddon started. Revelation 19:19 explains He will return to earth with the saints (armies) to go to war with the beast (Antichrist). In Revelation 19:11–16, there is proof of Jesus Christ's second coming.

I truly believe the reason why Christians misunderstand the second coming of Christ is because they don't read Bible prophecies in the books of Daniel and Revelation. The word *rapture* is nowhere in the Bible. Some Christians will say that in the tribulations, only the Jewish people will have a chance to receive salvation from God, our Lord and Savior, Jesus Christ. The Bible stated Jesus Christ is no respecter of person, and there is a Scripture that says that God gave His only begotten Son that whoever believes in Him shall not perish but will have eternal life. Then you have false prophets making false prophecies, predicting when Jesus Christ will return. On the other hand, you have people who think Jesus Christ will return secretly to rapture His saints. Why do people make false statements? Because they don't get an understanding on what the Bible says on this subject. Bible prophecies give an indication on Jesus's second coming to resurrect His saints and return to earth to battle Antichrist forces. People, it seems to me, don't believe in Bible prophecies anymore.

At the end of the age (the time of the end), Matthew 24:30–33 give specific events on when Jesus Christ's second coming is near. No, Christ didn't give a specific date on His return, but in the book of Matthew, chapter 24, it is self-explanatory. Christ told the disciples that there will be an increase of wars. There will be famines and pestilences and increase of earthquakes in divert places, but this is the beginning of sorrows. We always had wars, earthquakes, pestilences, and famines, but when we notice, these things will increase and really intensify. Take notice because the end of the world (age) is near. Major events are right around the corner because the great tribulation is closer than you think.

Revelation 19:11–16 explain nations will be gathered to fight against Jerusalem (Armageddon). This is when Jesus Christ returns with His saints. Zechariah 14:2–4 is about standing on Mount of Olives, God's enemies will be defeated. Antichrist and false prophet will be thrown in the lake of fire Revelation 19:20. Then Jesus will set up His kingdom on the earth.

So Jesus didn't give you the day or hour when He will return and resurrect His saints before. It's a true event that shows He had to resurrect them before He returns to earth with them to battle those armies that go against Jerusalem. Then His thousand-year reign will begin.

We, as children of God, must do all we can do with all our might to obtain the divine truth from God Himself. Ask Him for wisdom and understanding so we will not be so easily deceived by searching the Scriptures, praying earnestly, and studying the Bible like a king to receive a full understanding of His Word so we can heritage the kingdom of God.

I have a friend who's an elder in the Pentecost faith (I'm not picking on the Pentecost faith) in the year of 2019. We had a discussion on Jesus Christ's return to resurrect the saints; he believes that God will rapture the church before the start of the great tribulation. My friend said Jesus can come back at any time now. My response was Jesus Christ is not coming back this year nor the next year. He stated to me, "How do you know? Because He can come back at any time. He is not going to let His people suffer through the tribulation." I informed him that several events have to take place before the tribulation begins, and I said to him there is no such thing. The rapture is not in the Holy Scriptures. He stated to me that was my opinion and everybody has their own opinion. I then advised him I don't go by opinions but facts. I told him to read his Bible (study), basically, to really get a true understanding. This is one example how the people of God are being misled to the truth.

I believe wholeheartedly that the saints of God (some of them) doesn't study the books in the Bible concerning Bible prophecies; for instance, the books of Daniel, Ezekiel, Zechariah, and most of the book of Revelation of course. It's a shame because I truly believe of a great falling away in the last days before the Antichrist reveals himself. We, as saints of God, must view and study the Bible with an open mind. Without doing this, a person will never get a complete understanding of what the Bible is really telling us.

A person would be surprised what important information he or she could find in the so-called minor prophets' books—Zephaniah, Haggai, Malachi, Obadiah, Amos, Micah, Nahum, and Habakkuk. All these books have end-time messages. Several talks about a nuclear blast. Some may speak on the end-time church (lukewarm) and what will happen to them if they don't repent. For instance, take the book of Zephaniah, it talks about God's church law but mixing that law with pagan religion. God's holy days, Passover, unleavened bread, Pentecost, day of the trumpet, atonement, feast of tabernacle, and last great day are not to be mingled with the pagan days—New Year's, Valentine's, birthdays, Halloweens, Easters, and Christmases etc. God is not pleased.

The minor prophets, to me, are the major prophets too because they have a valuable message from God. Another book that I believe is an amazing book is the book of Habakkuk, which talks about Germany. The name Assyria today represents the nation of Germany. The Chaldeans, I believe, represent the Holy Roman Empire, which will be led by Germany. Germany and the Holy Roman Empire will be destroyed at the end-time. This book speaks about a nuclear blast that will happen. Read the book and get a full understanding on what's going to take place in the latter days. Also, books like Ezekiel, Isaiah, and Jeremiah speak about what major events will happen in the latter days. Ezekiel chapter 27 and Isaiah chapter 23 talk about mart of nations where countries of Europe, Russia, China, Greece, Japan, and others will create their own currency to get rid of the United States dollar. United States, because of this, will have an economic collapse. These books, as people think are just about history, but the Bible describe in detail what is going to occur in the latter days. A lot of people think nothing is going to happen to the United States, Israel, and Great Britain and other nations. God is a patient and loving God. He wants man to repent from their sins.

Some think some of these things will never happen.

"For the prophecy came not in old time by the will of man: but holy men of God spake as they were moved by the Holy Ghost" 2 Peter 1:21.

"For the vision is yet for an appointed time, but at the end it shall speak, and not lie: though it tarry, wait for it; because it will surely come, it will not tarry" Habakkuk 2:3 KJV.

Just like in the book of Genesis where Noah was warning the people on earth that a flood was coming, they didn't believe him at the end, and it was too late—people all died in the flood. Just like in the last days, which we are in now, destruction will come unaware. People will go about their daily lives not worrying about their salvation. Some may believe there is no God. God has a way of getting people's attention, and He will definitely do that. Well, I hope everyone that reads this book receives important understanding on what is going to happen when a person rejects God and what will happen if a person accepts God in their life. What is more important—this life of pleasure or being with God for eternity.

My suggestion is to get some good books to assist you in understanding what some words may mean and what they represent such as *Strong's Concordance*, *New International Version*, *New Living Translation*, and *The Bible: James Moffatt Translation with Concordance*—it's good those are good for the whole Bible. You must remember the Holy Bible is a Jewish book of Hebrew and Greek, it is not an American book—this is what the reader has to understand. Once a person realizes this, the Bible will be easier to study and understand. The person who studies the Bible with an open mind will find out some things they never knew that was there. They will be really surprised, so study hard and get an understanding.

Babylon is the country of Rome. The mother of harlots signifies the great city that rules over the kings of the earth (simplebible.com) *Abomination on the earth* is mainly used to denote idolatry, and in many other cases, it refers to inherently evil things such as illicit sex, lying, murder, deceit, and for unclean foods (google.com). "And upon her forehead was a name written, MYSTERY, BABYLON THE GREAT, THE MOTHER OF HARLOTS AND ABOMINATIONS OF THE EARTH. And I saw the woman drunken with the blood of the saints, and with the blood of the martyrs of Jesus: and when I saw her, I wondered with great admiration" Revelation 17:5–6 KJV. The word *harlot* is basically worshipping other gods (false). *Abomination* means, from *Oxford* dictionary, "a thing that causes disgust or hatred." The Antichrist will be controlled by the devil. He will have no respect for the true living God. The saints of God were killed because of their belief in Jesus Christ.

The mother of harlots is described in Revelation 17:3. John saw a woman (false churches) sit upon a scarlet-colored beast full of names of blasphemy having seven heads and ten horns. The false church will be very rich (wealthy). The seven heads represent the history of the Roman Empire. The seventh head will be the Antichrist (beast) in the last days having ten horns, which are ten kingdoms (government) that are under the beast. The saints were killed for not following the beast and false church agenda (one world government).

"And the angel said unto me, Wherefore didst thou marvel? I will tell thee the mystery of the woman, and of the beast that carrieth her, which hath the seven heads and ten horns. The beast that thou sawest was, and is not; and shall ascend out of the bottomless pit, and go into perdition: and they that dwell on the earth shall wonder, whose names were not written in the book of life from the foundation of the world, when they behold the beast that was, and is not, and yet is" Revelation 17:7–8 KJV. *Bottom pit*, as the *New Unger's*

Bible Dictionary explains it, is the pit of abyss, the prison house of demons. Right now, Germany is planning to take over the world sometime in the new future. They are doing things secretly, preparing for World War III.

This talks about the history of all the Roman empires that was established and has fallen but will ascend out of the bottomless pit (underground). The German people are secretly building their empire back up to power and the beast, he will go into perdition (destruction) to attempt to kill all the saints of God and those who oppose him. The last Roman Empire that was in operation was Germany in World War II under Hitler, and most people know the story about him. The one that is (and yet is) will be the new Roman Empire in the last days, which we are in this present time. He will cause so much havoc on earth as to what Hitler did in World War I and II; there will be no comparison to what he will do (beast).

"And there are seven kings: five are fallen, and one is, and the other is not yet come; an when he cometh, he must continue a short space" Revelation 17:10 KJV.

The beast and the false prophet will come and cause destruction to mankind, but they will only have a short time to this because when Jesus Christ comes again (second coming), He will destroy the Antichrist armies and throw the antichrist and the false prophet in the lake of fire alone.

"These shall make war with the Lamb, and the Lamb shall overcome them: for he is Lord of lords, and King of kings: and they that are with him are called, and chosen, and faithful" Revelation 17:14 KJV.

Jesus Christ is Lord and King. No one can oppose him; He is the ruler. Jesus Christ will strike the nations that fight against Jerusalem, and His saints will be with Him upon His second coming.

"And the fourth kingdom shall be strong as iron: forasmuch as iron breaketh in pieces and subdueth all things: and as iron that breaketh all these, shall it break in pieces and bruise" Daniel 2:40 KJV.

"And in the days of these kings shall the God of heaven set up a kingdom, which shall never be destroyed: and the kingdom shall not be left to other people, but it shall break in pieces and consume all these kingdoms, and it shall stand for ever" Daniel 2:44 KJV.

Jesus Christ will intervene and smash the beast system, and He (Christ) will set up His kingdom that will never be destroyed.

"Thus he said, The fourth beast shall be the fourth kingdom upon earth, which shall be diverse from all kingdoms, and shall devour the whole earth, and shall tread it down, and break it in pieces" Daniel 7:23 KJV.

"And the ten horns out of this kingdom are ten kings that shall arise; and another shall arise after them; and he shall be diverse from the first, and he shall subdue three kings" Daniel 7:24 KJV.

The ten horns (kings) will rise in the latter days, and he shall control the world under his system (control by force); the system will be the Holy Roman Empire.

ABOUT THE AUTHOR

My name is John Johnson. My foster parents were Pentecost faith Christians. They taught me about some things about the Bible. When I became a Christian, I served the lord in a lukewarm matter— not serious in serving the Lord. After rededicating myself to Christ, being devoted, I found out in the Bible that my foster parents misunderstood a couple of things pertaining to the Bible. My foster father would have discussions on the pre-Rapture (God will rapture his church before the tribulation begins. Rapture means Jesus Christ will return to earth before the great tribulation starts and take away all the saints that are alive so they will not face the wrath of the Antichrist and the wrath God will put on the earth for their wickedness. This is what most churches believe that will happen. This is not true. A person by the name of Maitland started this theory around the 1800s. Around 1820 to 1830, I believe. A man by the name of John Darby began this theory and convinced churches to believe in this concept. He thought during his time, the tribulation was about to happen, waiting for Jesus Christ to return and rapture the church. It didn't happen, so he came up with another idea that Jesus Christ can return at any time unexpectedly) by studying the Bible with an open mind. I found out that this is not true. Matthews 24 will give you a better understanding of the Resurrection. The Resurrection happens after the great tribulation, which is a seven-year period. First Thessalonians 4:16 says, "The Lord himself shall descend from heaven with a shout with the voice of the archangel and with the trump of God and the dead in Christ shall rise first." Verse 17 says, "Then we which are alive and remain shall be caught up together with him in the clouds to meet the Lord in the air and so shall we ever be with the Lord."

First Corinthians 15:51–52 says, "Behold, I show you a mystery we shall not all sleep but we shall all be changed. In a moment in the twinkling of an eye at the last trump for the trumpet shall sound and the dead shall raise incorruptible and we shall be changed." Verse 53 says, "For this corruptible must put on incorruption and this mortal [flesh and blood] must put on immortality [spiritual body]. First Corinthians 15:50 says, "Now this I say brethren that flesh and blood cannot inherit the kingdom of God neither doth corruption inherit incorruption [Jesus is going to transform our body into a glorified body spiritually]."

But make no mistake about it. My parents were good people. They were just confused about a couple of things. This is why a Christian should read the Bible for themselves to get the right understanding. I do have a certificate in studying Bible prophecy and other subjects pertaining to the Holy Bible. If a person would read the Bible and study it very carefully, the person will find out most of the prophets and disciples did not have any degrees to help them preach or teach about the Word of God. They were inspired by God to deliver the Word. Studying the Bible, a child can understand most of it because the Bible interprets itself. It's when people come up with their conclusions or own ideas on what some scriptures mean— this is why the world has some different beliefs about the Word of God. The devil is the main cause of this. Revelation 12:9 says, "He deceived the whole world. There are so many denominations it really is a shame." Ephesians 4:5–6 says, "There is one Lord one faith, one baptism One God and father of all, who is above all and through all, and in you all." But if a person would study the Bible—the books of Kings and Judges and the book of Samuel—they would notice that the prophets Samuel, Elijah, and Elisha had several colleges that taught about God's law, commandments, statues, and prophecy.